Animals of the Rainforest

Sloth

E. Melanie Watt

AV2

www.openlightbox.com

Step 1

Go to **www.openlightbox.com**

Step 2

Enter this unique code

KFAMSX26K

Step 3

Explore your interactive eBook!

AV2 is optimized for use on any device

Your interactive eBook comes with...

Contents
Browse a live contents page to easily navigate through resources

Audio
Listen to sections of the book read aloud

Videos
Watch informative video clips

Weblinks
Gain additional information for research

Slideshows
View images and captions

Try This!
Complete activities and hands-on experiments

Key Words
Study vocabulary, and complete a matching word activity

Quizzes
Test your knowledge

Share
Share titles within your Learning Management System (LMS) or Library Circulation System

Citation
Create bibliographical references following APA, CMOS, and MLA styles

This title is part of our AV2 digital subscription

1-Year Grades K–5 Subscription
ISBN 978-1-7911-3320-7

Access hundreds of AV2 titles with our digital subscription.
Sign up for a FREE trial at **www.openlightbox.com/trial**

The digital components of this book are guaranteed to stay active for at least five years from the date of publication.

Sloth

CONTENTS

Meet the Sloth

Sloths are slow-moving **mammals**. They have long limbs, furry bodies, and round heads. Sloths eat, sleep, rest, and are even born in trees.

Sloths may look similar to monkeys, but they are actually related to armadillos and anteaters. They have small ears and either short, stubby tails or no tail at all. Sloth claws are long and curved.

A Tropical Mammal

Sloths live in rainforests and other tropical forests of Central and South America. The six **species** of sloth are divided into two groups, based on how many claws they have on their front feet. The four three-toed species are smaller than the two species of two-toed sloths. Most sloths weigh about as much as a small dog.

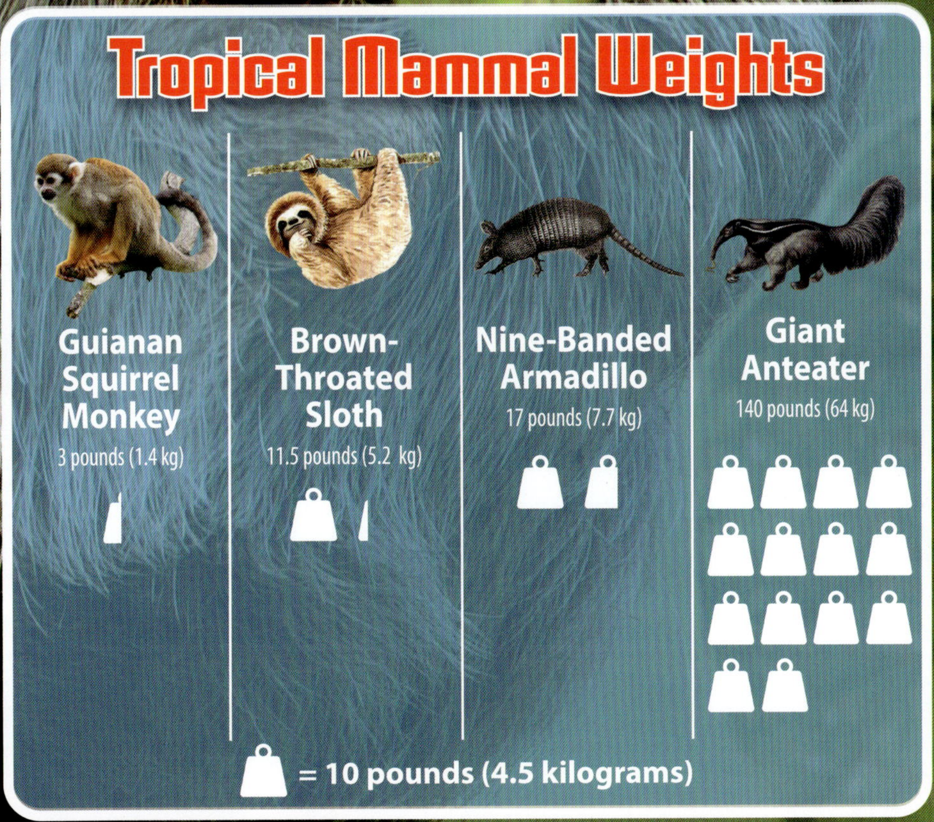

Solitary Sloths

Adult sloths live alone, unless they are females with young. Males will defend their **territories** from other males. Female sloths will do the same when encountering other females. When female sloths of some species are ready to find a **mate**, they make loud, whistle-like calls to attract males. However, the male sloth does not remain to help the mother raise her young.

If more than one male reaches a female sloth at the same time, the males may fight to decide which one becomes her mate.

Growing Up

A mother sloth gives birth while hanging from a tree. The one newborn sloth, or pup, clings to its mother's chest. It drinks small amounts of milk at a time. When it is about a week old, the pup begins to lick food from its mother's mouth. Soon after that, it starts to eat leaves. After 5 weeks to 5 months, depending on the species, the mother and pup will begin to move apart.

SLOTH FACT

The typical lifespan of a two-toed sloth is about **20 years**.

A Closer Look

Sloths have **adapted** to their **habitats**. They have unique features that help them survive in their environment.

Fur

Sloths have an outer layer of thick, long fur. It can be different shades of brown to gray. **Algae**, lice, moths, and other living things make their homes in sloth fur.

Neck

Three-toed sloths have more neck **vertebrae** than many other mammals. This allows them to turn their heads almost all the way around.

Claws

Both two- and three-toed sloths have long, sharp claws on each front foot. Sloths use these claws to grip trees, eat, and defend themselves.

Limbs

A sloth's long limbs help it hang and move through trees. Sloths are clumsy on the ground, using their limbs to pull themselves along.

Teeth

A sloth's teeth are always growing. They are worn down when the animal chews on plants, stopping them from becoming too long.

Blending In

Sloths are well **camouflaged** in their natural environment. The algae that grows on their fur gives it a greenish appearance. This coloring helps sloths blend in well with the branches and green leaves around them. It is difficult for **predators**, such as jaguars and eagles, to spot them in trees. Moving very slowly also helps sloths stay hidden.

Due to their slow speed, sloths usually only move a distance of about 125 feet (38 meters) each day.

Slowing Down

A sloth's diet does not give it a large amount of energy. Sloths can survive on this diet because their bodies save energy. Part of this is because the animals move very slowly through trees. In addition, sloth bodies save more energy by taking days or even weeks to **digest** food. Sloths move slowly on the ground, and usually only leave trees to get rid of waste. However, sloths are strong swimmers. They can swim three times faster in the water than they move on land.

SLOTH FACT

Some sloth species can hold their breath underwater for about **40 minutes**.

A Tree-Bound Diet

Sloths find their food by touch and smell. Once they have located food on a nearby branch, they use their long, curved claws to pull it down to their mouths. Sloths mainly eat plant material, including leaves, buds, sap, and fruit. Some will also eat animal matter, such as insects or bird eggs.

Sloths get water from their food or by licking dew drops off leaves and fruit.

Sloth

Sloth Conservation

Threats to sloths include habitat loss, often caused by the construction of roads. Sloths can only cross roads slowly, making them vulnerable to traffic. This has led to several sloth species becoming **endangered**. As sloths live in trees, they need healthy tropical forests to survive. Many countries have taken steps to preserve natural forests. Some conservation groups help sloths by building rope bridges between forested areas, allowing sloths to travel between them safely.

Pygmy three-toed sloths are only found on one small island off the coast of Panama.

Sloth Conservation Status

EX	EW	CR	EN	VU	NT	LC
Extinct	Extinct in the Wild	Critically Endangered	Endangered	Vulnerable	Near Threatened	Least Concern
		Pygmy Three-Toed Sloth		Maned Three-Toed Sloth		Brown-Throated Sloth

Sloth Quiz

1
How many claws does a sloth have on each of its front feet?

2
Which other animals are closely related to sloths?

3
How many species of sloth are there?

4
How many young does a mother sloth have at a time?

5
How far do sloths typically move each day?

6
How quickly can sloths swim?

7
What is the typical lifespan of a two-toed sloth?

8
What makes a sloth's fur look green?

ANSWERS **1.** Either two or three, depending on the species **2.** Armadillos and anteaters **3.** Six **4.** One **5.** About 125 feet (38 meters) **6.** Three times faster than they move on land **7.** About 20 years **8.** Algae

Key Words

adapted: changed to suit the environment

algae: plant-like living things, such as seaweed and lichen

camouflaged: hidden by matching one's background

digest: break down food to obtain energy

endangered: in danger of no longer surviving in the world

habitats: places where animals live, grow, and raise their young

mammals: warm-blooded animals that have hair and nurse their young

mate: a member of a pair of animals that have young

predators: animals that hunt other animals for food

species: a group of related living things that can reproduce

territories: home areas that animals will defend from intruders

vertebrae: small bones which are stacked together to form the neck and spine

Index

Get the best of both worlds.

AV2 bridges the gap between print and digital.

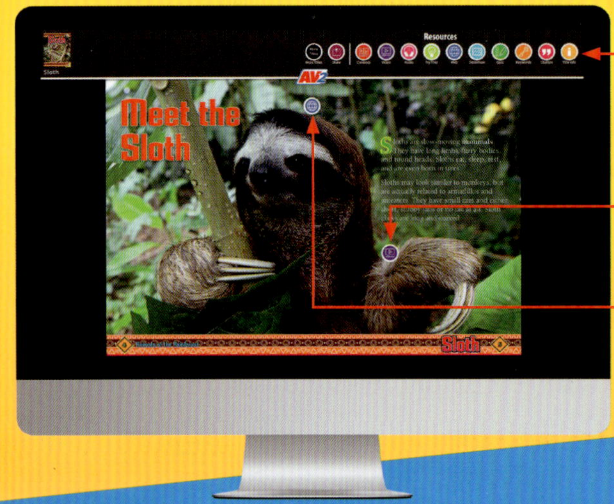

The expandable resources toolbar enables quick access to content including **videos**, **audio**, **activities**, **weblinks**, **slideshows**, **quizzes**, and **key words**.

Animated videos make static images come alive.

Resource icons on each page help readers to further **explore key concepts**.

Published by Lightbox Learning Inc.
276 5th Avenue, Suite 704 #917
New York, NY 10001
Website: www.openlightbox.com

Library of Congress Control Number: 2023939840

ISBN 978-1-7911-5736-4 (hardcover)
ISBN 978-1-7911-5737-1 (softcover)
ISBN 978-1-7911-5738-8 (multi-user eBook)

082023
101122

Printed in Guangzhou, China
1 2 3 4 5 6 7 8 9 0 27 26 25 24 23

Project Coordinator: Priyanka Das
Art Director: Terry Paulhus

Every reasonable effort has been made to trace ownership and to obtain permission to reprint copyright material. The publisher would be pleased to have any errors or omissions brought to its attention so that they may be corrected in subsequent printings.

The publisher acknowledges Alamy, Dreamstime, Getty Images, Minden Pictures, and Shutterstock as its primary image suppliers for this title.